The Bible ABCs

Learning About The Bible with Help from the ABCs

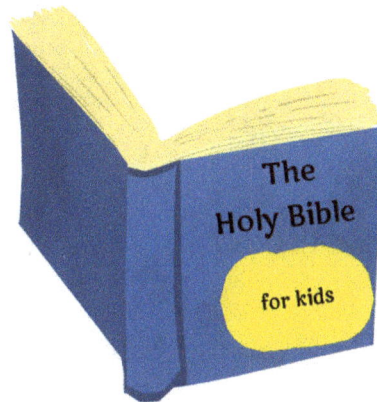

The
Holy Bible

for kids

by:

Freddy Allen Barron Sr.

Illustrated by:
Hatice Bayramoglu

Printed in the United States of America.
First Printing, May 2021
ISBN: 978-1-7371761-1-4 (Paperback)

Author: Freddy Barron Sr.
Illustrator: Hatice Bayramoglu
Editor: Tamira K. Butler-Likely
Assisted by: Write It Out Publishing LLC

https://www.freddybarron.com/

Dedication

This book is dedicated to my children: Janessa, Jasmine, Fiona, Daniel, Freddy Jr., and Arilla. I love you all so very much!

Special thanks and shout outs to all my family and friends. To my wife, Tahrita, I love you very much! To my grandparents, Elder Emmanuel Barron & Evangelist Arilla Mae Barron, I love you both always & forever. Gone but never forgotten! To my mother, Lynn, I love you! To my father, Apostle Carlos Keith, I love you! To all my siblings, I thank God for you all and love you very much! To everyone that has impacted my life in some special way, and you know who you are, I say thank you! I love you and appreciate each and every one of you! God bless you all!

FOREWORD

One of the first songs that a child learns when he/she is young is the ABC (or alphabet) song. It is simple, it is memorable, it is teachable, and it remains with them for a lifetime. If your child is anything like my two-year-old daughter, once she learned it, she sang it over and over again. Children don't understand the importance of the alphabet song; to them, it is just a song to sing. But there is so much more to the song that will help them in their educational journey.

For me, education is extremely important; I am a pre-k teacher, a former Sunday school teacher, and a children's church teacher at my church. So, as you can see, it doesn't matter if they are being taught in a school or at church; children need to understand and realize that education is the key to life. They will get this understanding from their first teachers, their parents. Parents can lead and teach their children the fundamentals at home so when they attend school and/or church, they will be able to use what their parents have taught them to build upon in their education. Being a mother of two young daughters, I want to keep education a priority for them, academically and spiritually. My husband and I are teaching them the fundamentals now, so it won't be difficult when they begin to attend school.

Academically, the ABCs are a very essential part of a child's development. In learning the alphabet, a child can identify as well as learn the sound of each letter (phonemic awareness), they will later learn how to put letters together to make words, and ultimately, they will learn how to read. As a result, teaching ABCs helps children in many ways in reading fundamentals.

Just as it is important for children to learn for reading purposes, it is also more important for children to learn about the Bible for life purposes. In the Bible, there is a message for children who experience life situations and what better way to learn both at the same time than by reading this book, The Bible ABCs: Learning About the Bible with Help from the ABCs. This book encompasses the basics of the Bible, on a child's level, while learning the alphabet.

In conclusion, the ABCs have meaning in both a child's academic and spiritual life. Academically, it will help them to identify letters, make words, and eventually read. Spiritually, they will be able to read the word of God and apply it to their everyday life. This book will help children in both areas; they will be able to learn about and read the word of God while learning the ABCs. Take a moment, read this book and enhance your child's knowledge of the alphabet and the Bible.

Written by Jomeica Rambert

I can do all things through Christ
who strengthens me.

Philippians 4:13 NKJV

The Bible ABCs

Learning About The Bible with Help from the ABCs

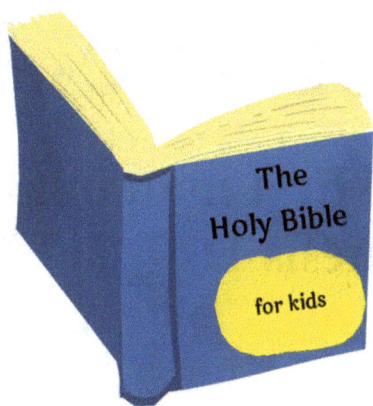

The
Holy Bible

for kids

by:

Freddy Allen Barron Sr.

Illustrated by:
Hatice Bayramoglu

A is for the Adam!

Adam was the first man in all of the world:
Genesis 1:27, 2:7 NLT

B is for the Bible!

The scriptures in the Bible are inspired by God: 2 Timothy 3:16 NLT

C is for Christ!

Jesus was referred to as the Christ by Simon Peter: Matthew 16:16 KJV

D is for Daniel!

Daniel was cast into the lions' den:
Daniel 6:16 KJV

E is for Eve!

Eve was the first woman in all of the world:
Genesis 1:27, 2:21-23 NLT

F is for Faith!

Without faith, it is impossible to please God: Hebrews 11:6 NLT

FAITH

G is for Goliath!

Goliath was the BIG giant who was slain by David: 1 Samuel 17:41-51 KJV

His for Heaven!

Heaven is where God resides and where we want to spend eternity: Revelation 21:3-4 NLT

I is for Isaac!

Isaac was the promised son to Abraham and Sarah. They birthed Isaac at a very old age: Genesis 21:1-3 NLT

J is for Jesus!

Jesus was born to save the world from their sins: Matthew 1:21 NLT

K is for Kind!

Be kind to each other: Ephesians 4:32 NLT

KIND

L is for Love!

Love is the greatest: 1 Corinthians 13:13 NLT

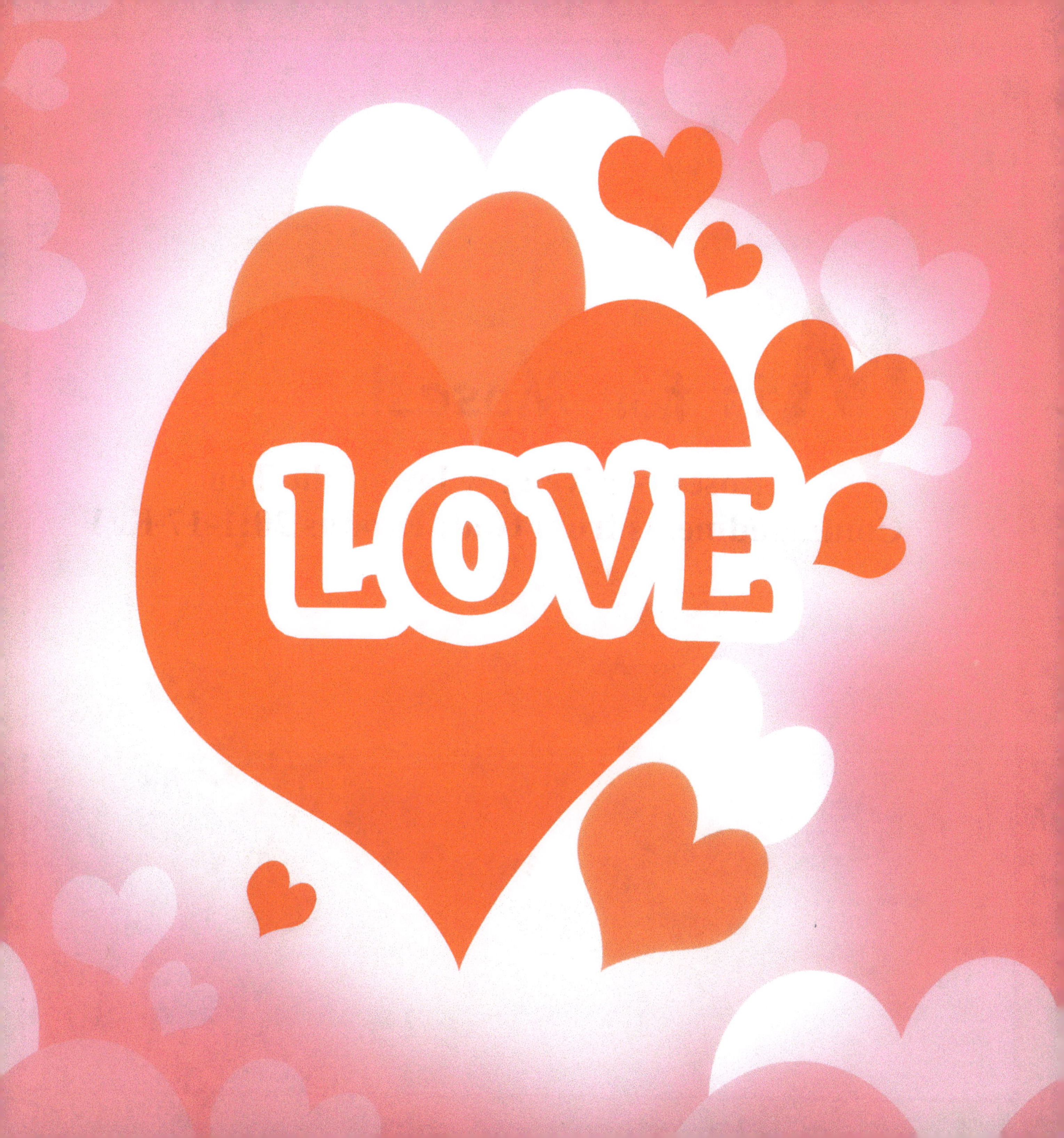
LOVE

M is for Moses!

Moses received the law of the Ten Commandments from God: Exodus 20:1-17 KJV

N is for Neighbor!

**Love your neighbor as you love yourself:
Galatians 5:14 NLT**

O is for Obey!

Children, obey your parents in the Lord, for this is right: Ephesians 6:1 KJV

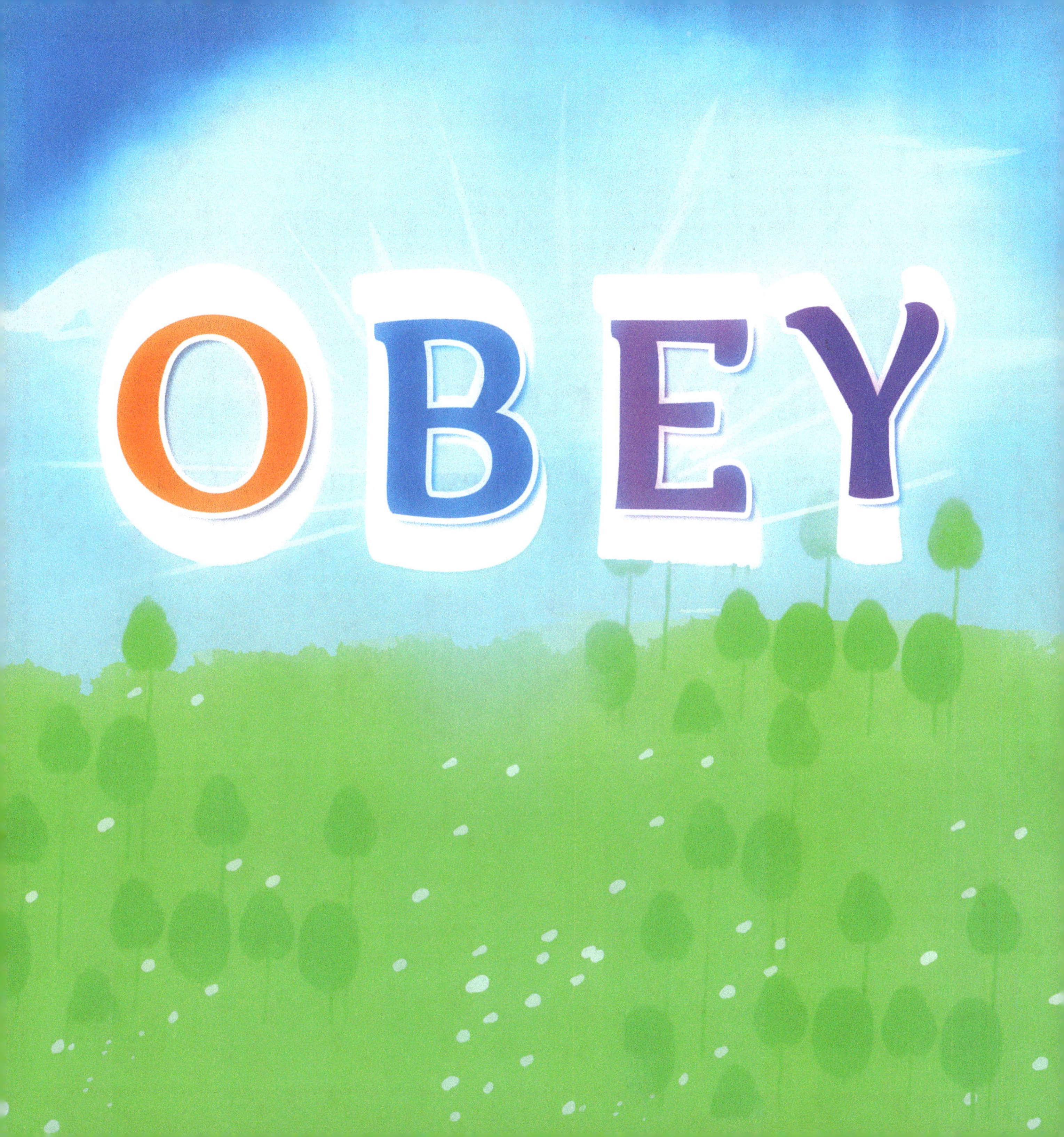
OBEY

P is for Praying!

Never stop praying: 1 Thessalonians 5:17 NLT

Q is for Queen Esther!

Esther became queen: Esther 2:17 NLT

R is for Resurrection!

Jesus is the resurrection and the life: John 11:25 NLT

Resurrection

S is for Samson!

Samson was known as the strongest man in the Bible: Judges 14 & 15 KJV

T is for Trust!

Trust in the Lord with all your heart:
Proverbs 3:5 NLT

TRUST

U is for Unity!

It is beautiful when there is unity among God's people: Psalms 133:1 NLT

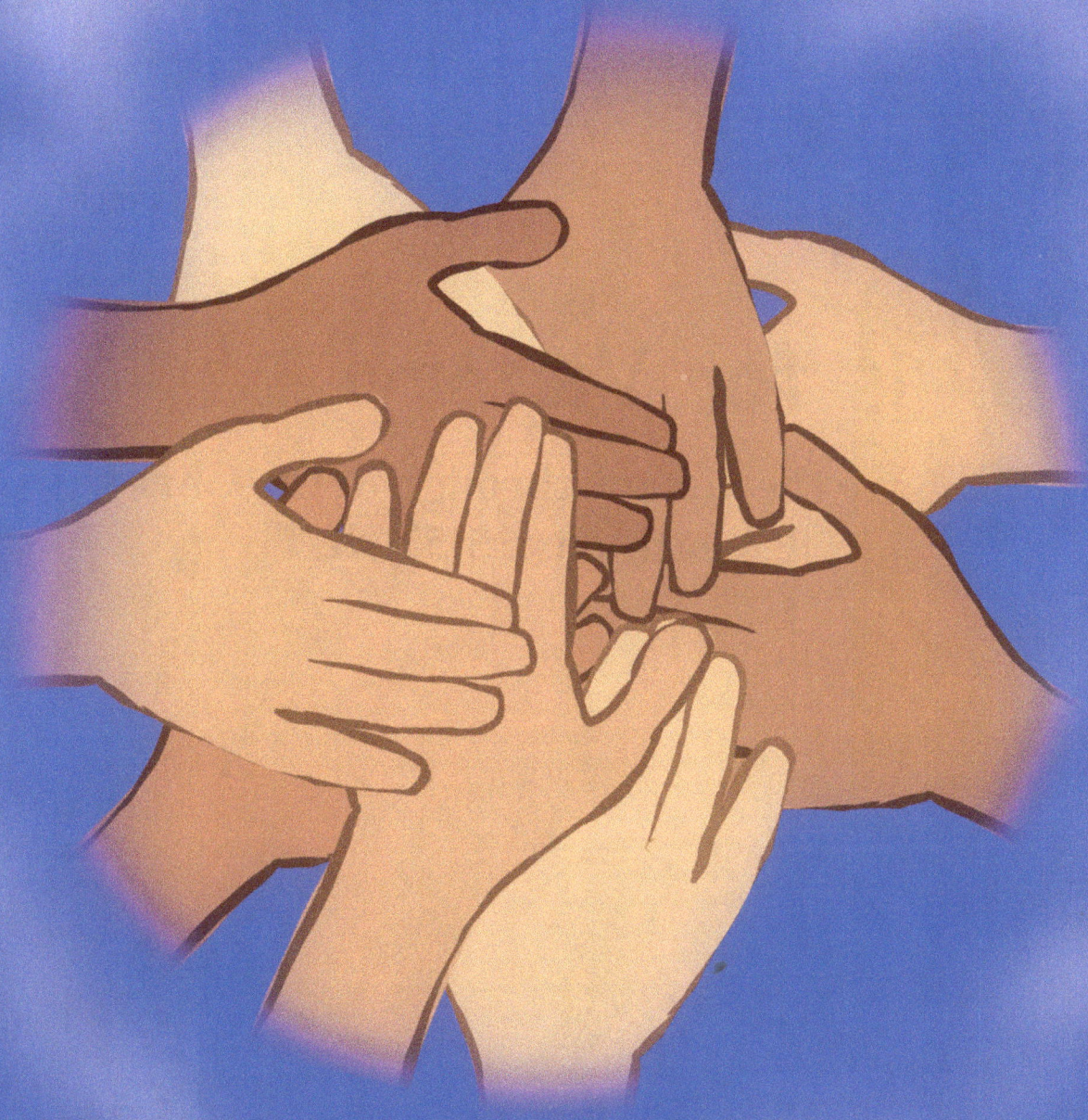

V is for Victory!

We have the victory through Jesus Christ: 1 Corinthians 15:57 NLT

VICTORY

W is for Worship!

God is spirit. Those who worship him must worship in spirit and truth: John 4:24 NLT

X is for Xerxes!

Xerxes was another name for the king who made Esther the queen: Esther 2:16-17 NLT

Y is for You!

Jesus said: You should love the Lord your God with all your heart, soul, and mind: Matthew 22:37 NLT

YOU

Z is for Zion!

Zion is referred to the spiritual city where God's people live with him: Revelation 14:1 NLT

ZION

Congratulations! You have learned your ABCs
and also discovered 26 interesting facts
from the Bible. Can you recite your
ABCs now on your own? If not, let's read this
book again and again!